To Bill and
May you deeply know
God's rest.
Love,

DESPERATE REST: RESTORING YOUR SOUL THROUGH SABBATICAL

First edition. July 11, 2018.

Copyright © 2018 Laura Demetrician, LMFT.
ISBN: 9781717847980

Written by Laura Demetrician, LMFT

Desperate Rest

Restoring Your Soul Through Sabbatical

I dedicate this book to those who are burnt-out
and desperate for peace.
May you know that the One who loves you
longs to draw you into rest.

6

Table of Contents

8

Introduction

10

Matthew 11:28-30

Come to me, all you who are weary and burdened,
and I will give you rest. Take my yoke upon you
and learn from me, for I am gentle and humble in heart,
and you will find rest for your souls.
For my yoke is easy and my burden is light.

It was a snowy, bitterly cold Wisconsin day in a nature preserve. I picked up the phone and told my husband I needed a break, an extended break.

My husband, Adam, is a pastor. And that makes me a pastor's wife. You probably know it's a rough place to be when the pastor's wife needs a break.

Over the previous months, I problem-solved, grasped, and wracked my brain to find the solution to my exhaustion. I went on retreats. I prioritized my time. I spent extended hours with the Lord. Yet the strength I needed slipped through my fingers over and over again. Every attempt I made plunged me further into a deep frustration at my inability to fix my exhausted state. I felt emotionally raw. It was as if I might bleed with one more tug of stress, expectation, or difficulty. I was beyond tired, and I was at a loss at what to do. I felt pulled in a million directions, as if I didn't have control of my life.

Twenty years ago I felt called into church ministry, but it hadn't turned out like I imagined. When Adam and I fell in love at Bible College, we dreamed of a life of adventure, friendships, family, and community impact. We had the beginnings that most pastors would dream of. We had energy. We had faithful friends. We had an excellent education. Adam had ideal opportunities at vibrant churches.

Adam began working at churches in official capacities and I stayed home fulltime with our children.

I sensed my calling to vocational ministry when I was just 17 years old on a missions trip to the Philippines. I was a brand new Christian when a last-minute spot opened up for me to join a team from my youth group and journey to the Philippines. We held church services in busy town squares, visited small congregations in remote tropical locations, assisted in programs for undernourished children, and worshipped for hours in urban churches with the most heavenly-focused people I had ever met. We went to a garbage dump where I held a dying baby. We sang songs, gave encouragement to congregations, and loved and hugged on children. After only knowing God intimately for just a few months, there was no doubt how I was supposed to spend my life.

I made plans to attend Bible College after I graduated from high school. I was boldly confident as to the general direction of my life, but I was equally confused about the details. During my time at Southeastern University, I looked around at my classmates. Most of the students displayed the spiritual gifts of leadership, administration, and teaching. It was a challenge to understand my calling when my spiritual gifts of wisdom and discernment didn't naturally flow into job categories such as "youth pastor" or "associate pastor." I could sense that I was different, and confusion set in.

I met Adam as a freshman my first day on campus. He was so confident and intelligent. Our first class together was Public Speaking. The best speaker in the class, he was the bar the rest of us measured ourselves by. His calm, confident presence was far different from my shaky and scared presentation. He was kind of a dork, though. Most Friday and Saturday nights our friends would find him in the library and convince him to come out with us.

Our friendship began with mutual admiration for wanting to love and serve God. And I thought he was the best looking guy in the world. We talked and talked about what we wanted in life. We walked around the beautiful lakes by our college. We exercised together. We studied together. And it was no longer than a year of dating that we knew we wanted to spend our lives together.

Once we were engaged, Adam and I simply didn't know how our vocations and careers would work together. Our graduation from college was approaching and we were planning our wedding and frantically making plans for graduate school. The reality that there are few church positions available for couples set fear in our decisions. We both got scared. We let fear win. We decided that I should study psychology and forgo plans to enter into vocational church ministry.

One would think that a husband and wife who both wanted to work in vocational ministry would have an easy time finding work, but that wasn't our reality.

I laid my dreams on the altar of what "made sense."

That fork in the road was the biggest mistake of my life. That sabotaging decision led to years of repeatedly and dutifully laying down my dreams and deference to my husband's calling.

I spent those years unhappily living my decisions based on Adam's work and it was killing me and our marriage. I had been told, verbally and implicitly by many people, that Adam's ministry was more important. The visibility of Adam's spiritual gifts of leadership and teaching had always been more evident than my own spiritual gifts of wisdom and discernment. My own lack of self-worth kept me from being strong enough to reject those lies.

I twice gave up jobs and even a business so that my husband could pursue his ministry dreams. I kept holding out hope that someday it would be my turn. Little by little, I shut my heart down to not feel the pain of being a victim of my own sabotage.

Standing outside on that blustery day in the nature preserve, I realized that I had strayed so far from what that 20-year-old girl had dreamed, and I needed to fix it. And it couldn't wait another minute. That wedge in my own soul and in our marriage led me to the place of needing desperate rest.

Why had I believed the lie that my calling was less significant than Adam's?

Why didn't we fight to pursue my dreams?

I needed space to work through two decades of damage. The choices Adam and I made put a wedge between us. It eroded at the trust between us. The lie that I was not important or called dug a deep root in my soul. Healing damage that deep would take work. It would also take a time away.

When God is moving, calling, inspiring, and lovingly awakening people, the enemy also begins working. I allowed the weapons of insecurity and doubt to wound my dreams. Over the course of many crucial and minor decisions, I had little by little put my dreams, hopes, and ideas of the future to sleep.

They didn't die, though.

God-given dreams don't die. And if they seem dead, God will continually awaken them. He did with me. He will do the same with you.

God displayed His love and patience with me. He used my exhaustion to wear me down. I had no choice but to go to the source of my pain, and the only answer I could imagine was for me to take a step back with a sabbatical. My soul was sick of my sabotage, and it finally screamed loud enough for my deaf ears to listen.

There were other factors that led to my exhaustion.
At the time of my sabbatical, we had served in 4 churches in 4 different

states in 14 years. In all of our moves, we had been out of one church and in another the next week. We had enough time to get our boxes in our home before jumping into meeting new people and starting a new life. We have only taken a couple two-week vacations. The only breaks I took were after the births of our daughters.

It was time for me to have some breathing room for God to heal my wounds and start creating healthier patterns.

I wasn't aware of how cruel I had been to myself when I started my sabbatical. That realization was a process that was crafted in the soul space that my sabbatical provided. It was a process of tears, freedom, painful self-realization, whispers of the Holy Spirit, input from others, and time.

I am hoping this book will help you to take a step back and evaluate your need for breathing room.

I hope that in sharing my story that it will help you to look at the rhythms of your life. I pray that you will listen upward (to God) and inward (to your own heart) and truthfully ask if a break could be a time of obedience, rest, and delight.

Not all sabbaticals start with a crisis or exhaustion. It actually shouldn't be that way. I would love to see sabbaticals become a routine part of the rhythm in the lifetime of pastors and their families. And I would love to help others take action before burnout.

The strange thing is that a pastor's wife sabbatical should not be a shocking scandal. The spouse of a paid spiritual leader and shepherd, who volunteers their time to care, sacrifice, and shoulder the burdens of others, should feel the freedom to take a break. Pastors' spouses usually do this with no pay for his/her work, experience, education, expertise, and heart for people.

There is an aspect about being a pastor's wife that I have never heard anyone speak about, yet I know that many experience it. It is a kind of powerlessness. Pastor's wives move for their husband's calling. Many bring a unique education, experience, expertise, and heart for people, and are asked to volunteer. In doing this for decades, we are left with no relevant resume' information or pension. Our labor is one of the heart, and it gets hurt. A pastor's wife's schedule is dictated by the church calendar that we rarely are in control of scheduling. We take the kids to piano lessons because our husband is at a church event or meeting, and then we are criticized for not being around. Pastor's wives do not regularly make decisions in the church, yet are faced with defending them to others, even when we may actually disagree with the decision at hand.

I could keep going on and on. I could talk about the emotionally taxing nature of being available for congregations' most urgent needs, intense traumas, and grief. I could talk about the need to be spiritually strong not only for your family, but for many others. I could write a whole book about this, but I imagine you already know it.

Being a pastor's wife is challenging. This isn't just me, right? Whether you are on staff at the church, or your husband is the lead pastor, or the youth pastor's wife, the stress of ministry affects you.

I will ask you this. Do you create space to rest?

In this book, you will find the story of my sabbatical. I share my story in an attempt to inspire you to take stock of your rhythms of rest. My story may only resemble yours in bits and pieces, but we can always learn from one another. We are made too wonderfully by the Creator to ignore our own souls.

In this book, you will also find a practical guide to taking a sabbatical. I feel passionate about sabbaticals for pastors' wives because I have seen the struggle of many. I have experienced the battle myself. And I had the beautiful experience of being formed and shaped in ways that I couldn't have predicted.

Intentional rest, with the focus on the presence of Christ, not only impacts our own soul, but our marriage, our family, and the church we serve. Ministry is not always one continual marathon. Sometimes it is a series of races. In between these sprints of ministry challenges, seasons of the year, and marathons of long-term visions, we need rest.

It took exhaustion and frustration for me to enter the gift of sabbatical. I did not anticipate the beauty, the insight, and the fruit that would emerge. I began it out of desperation, and I exited with soul insight, healing, and personal vision that only rest and space can provide.

So grab a journal. Journey with me as we process.

. . . .

Note: I will, for ease of writing and reading, use the words "pastor's wife" and the pronouns "her, she." There are many incredible male spouses of female pastors and leaders. I will love it if they read this book. There is a reality, though, that more is expected of pastor's wives than pastor's husbands. Pastor's husbands tend to experience more freedom to pursue dreams and more independence given to church involvement. If I am wrong in that opinion, I welcome a conversation!

Chapter 1

A Pastor's Wife Sabbatical?

The Role of a Pastor's Wife

What a strange role. What a strange life it is.

Being a witness to miraculous life change is exhilarating.

Our hearts are broken when we are betrayed.

We get to be a small part of God moving here on earth.

And we are also cut off at the knees by gossip that we cannot defend.

We are given responsibility but not really an authorized, voted-in, or hired on position;
a role, but only because of a relationship;
a voice, and sometimes great influence;
expectations, some stated and some unspoken;
and an honor to be present in the sacred, devastating, and beautiful moments of people's lives.

In the beauty and the burden, sometimes we need a break.

Think what you want, but being a pastor's spouse is weird. Some love us just because we are married to the pastor. We get scowled at because someone is furious at our husband for a reason we don't even know about. We experience vacations that are interrupted and cut short because of deaths and tragedies. We sit alone at our kids' games that our spouses miss because they are meeting with a couple on the verge of a divorce.

There are enormous expectations on pastors and their spouses that are unknown when we enter the ministry. We hold and bear the stress of the church and ministry in our homes. If there is a crisis in the church (and when isn't there some kind of emergency in the church?), then it is felt in our home. It all rests in our home. We know things about people's lives and situations that are difficult. We struggle with what and when and if to say something that we think/know/want.

We bear a burden of protecting our children from all of this stress, not wanting the weight of ministry to scar their relationship with God and His Church. We have a husband that we share; and sometimes we don't want to share him.

Don't even get me started on times that I was mortified by something my husband has said from the stage! I should have kept a record of all of the things that made me want to shrink down in my seat.

Maybe the most intangible weight is the overall spiritual and relational weight of the challenges that settle in our home whether we recognize them or not.

Pastors' spouses spend hours and hours providing a listening ear and reflecting on the problems in the church. Our family conversations are interrupted to take a call from a board member, staff member, or person in crisis. We feel the pressure to always look "put together" (Although I have given up trying to live up to that pressure). We receive criticism for everything you can imagine and then some.

I say these things not to gain pity, or to ask for affirmation. The churches we have served in have been loving and accepting. My husband and I chose this life as much as we were called to it. I can't imagine any other way of living. I say these things because taking a break from this role can be marriage-saving, ministry-making, and soul-healing.

There is no manual or "10 Steps to Being a Perfect Pastors' Wife." Every individual, marriage, church, stage of life, and calling should lead to a different result. Our goal is to live our lives in obedience to God.

Too many women live out their life as a pastor's wife from the expectations of others. Blind duty, resigned obligation, and unsaid and spoken expectations form a stronghold that smothers freedom and obedience. It's time for something different.

My Story

I have never heard of a pastor's wife taking a sabbatical by herself. I knew female pastors who had created sabbatical time. I knew pastor's wives who took a sabbatical with their husbands.

So I knew for our church and me, this was new ground. And breaking new ground in the church can be scary.

I consider myself to be a logical person. But sometimes I am naïve and get blindsided when I don't anticipate the reactions of others who don't see things the same way. Maybe they disagree with my logic, or perhaps it goes against their prior experience.

When making decisions, convention, tradition, and people's opinion should not dictate what we do. The above is to be consulted, but they are not to be the sole guide of one's choices. Just because something is uncommon does not mean that it is not valid, necessary, or essential. Our decisions should be brought before God. Sometimes He speaks to us, and we know it is His voice. And sometimes God speaks through the longings of our heart. And sometimes we just do the best we know how.

Here was my logic and how I came to the conclusion that I would take a break. I try to think about the big picture when I make decisions. I consider not only the different parts of the system, but the whole timeline in years and months. I think about the whole system when I think about the church. I consider the different relationships and history when I think about our family. And now when I contemplate my goals, needs, and decisions, I see my life as a timeline from birth to death.

I hope for a long life to retirement age and beyond. I envision 40 years of church ministry with Adam. I see raising the girls in the midst of this time (with the sacrifice and craziness that accompany those years). I then see sending them off to college at a relatively young age, as we had them pretty young. And I viewed my sabbatical in the timeline of my life.

I realized that we were nearly halfway through our ministry career. And therefore, I realized that three months in the context of 40 years of service is not a large percentage. And I saw a three-month break from ministry as an entirely reasonable thing to do.

But this wasn't exactly how everyone else viewed it; and here is the awkward reality of where being a pastor's wife met my logic. I am not an employee of the church, yet I have obligations. I had no official role

other than the fact that I am married to the pastor, and yet some
people did not react well to my sabbatical.

For many years, I loved the role and relationship. It was a privilege to
be the one that was called upon for input and prayer. It was a gift to see
a couple journey from crisis to restoration to helping other couples. I
enjoyed being a small voice in the process of important decisions.

But when I needed a break, the role became a burden, and it was
suffocating. I didn't want to hurt anyone, most of all Pathways Church
as a whole. What was I to do?

What Is A Sabbatical?

The root word of sabbatical is "Sabbath." Let's first explore some
biblical texts about Sabbath and Sabbatical years.

There is no biblical command that declares that pastors must take
sabbaticals, but there are many passages that point to God
commanding rest for his creation. I believe that the biblical concepts of
Sabbath and Sabbatical years lead us to the fact that God doesn't LET
us enjoy rest, but He WANTS us to enjoy rest. In fact, the passages
below demonstrate punishment for when Sabbath isn't kept.

In the longest of the Ten Commandments, God gave us the commandment of Sabbath.

Exodus 20: 8-11 (NIV)

Remember to keep the Sabbath day holy. Do all your work in six days. But the seventh day is a Sabbath to honor the Lord your God. Do not do any work on that day. The same command applies to your sons and daughters, your male and female servants, and your animals. It also applies to any outsiders who live in your towns. In six days the Lord made the heavens, the earth, the sea and everything in them. But he rested on the seventh day. So the Lord blessed the Sabbath day and made it holy.

God includes more explanation in this command than any other commandment. And He does this to show his heart for His people. It was a reminder that Israel was no longer slaves in a foreign land. His people were His sons and daughters, and they were journeying to their Promise Land.

Exodus 31:15-17 (NIV)

For six days, work is to be done, but the seventh day is a Sabbath of rest, holy to the Lord. Whoever does any work on the Sabbath day must be put to death. The Israelites are to observe the Sabbath, celebrating it for the generations to come as a lasting covenant. It will be a sign between me and the Israelites forever, for in six days the Lord made the heavens and the earth, and on the seventh day he abstained from work and rested.

This is the basis, the foundation for all believers regarding rest. Sabbath is the one day a week where we cease work to show our dependence on God, to delight in God, and to honor Him.

Oh, how we are so disobedient to it! Forgive us, Lord. We run from the good gift that God has for us.

There is so much beauty in these texts. The Sabbath is a sign. It is a representation of the covenant and a reminder that we are not slaves. He commands us to rest so that we remember who we are. The Sabbath is a sign that God doesn't need us to do everything. The Sabbath displays that we should not be slaves to our work, even good work, even ministry.

When the people of Israel were new in their freedom from their oppressors, the Egyptians, God gave them instructions on many things. One of these instructions was the very rarely talked about Sabbath Year:

Exodus 23:10-11 (NIV)

For six years you are to sow your fields and harvest the crops, but
during the seventh year let the land lie unplowed and unused.
Then the poor among your people may get food from it, and the wild
animals may eat what they leave.
Do the same with your vineyard and olive grove.

After wandering in the desert for 40 years, God reminded the people:

Leviticus 25:1-7 (NIV)

The Lord said to Moses on Mount Sinai, 'speak to the Israelites and
say to them; When you enter the land I am going to give you, the land
itself must observe a Sabbath to the Lord. For six years sow your fields,
and for six years prune your vineyards and gather their crops. But in
the seventh year, the land is to have a Sabbath of rest, a Sabbath to the
Lord. Do not sow your fields or prune your vineyards. Do not reap
what grows of itself or harvest the grapes of your untended vines. The
land is to have a year of rest. Whatever the land yields during the
Sabbath year will be food for you – for yourself, your manservant and
maidservant, and the hired worker and temporary resident who live

among you, as well as for your livestock and the wild animals in your
land. Whatever the land produces may be eaten.

Why would God ask Israel to rest the land?

We can see the evidence in non-stop use of land in our modern
farming. (The constant push to produce more, the dwindling of
nutrients in the soil, the take, take, take from the land: it all leads to
depletion. The land yields less.) It is the same with our souls.

Sabbath is not a luxury or a "right" to be fought for. It is not a privilege
that is earned. Sabbath is a command.

Mark Buchanan, in his book *The Rest of God: Restoring Your Soul by*
Restoring Sabbath, writes:

> "In a culture where busyness is a fetish and stillness is
> laziness, rest is sloth. But without rest, we miss the rest
> of God: the rest he invites us to enter more fully so that
> we might know him more deeply. 'Be still, and know
> that I am God.' Some knowing is never pursued, only
> received. And for that, you need to be still. Sabbath is
> both a day and an attitude to nurture such stillness. It is
> both time on a calendar and disposition of the heart. It

is a day we enter, but just as much a way we see. Sabbath
imparts the rest of God; actual physical, mental, spiritual
rest, but also the rest of God, the things of God, nature
and presence we miss in our busyness."

There is no biblical mandate for pastors, or spouses, or people to take
sabbaticals, but there are biblical themes that, when followed, lead to
fruit that only rest and space can provide.

All you need to do is to speak to a burnt-out, tired pastor who is
preaching 50 weeks a year BEFORE and AFTER a 3-month
sabbatical. That pastor will be different. It is the difference between
frazzled and present, on-edge and rested, empty and full. The
correlation of what sabbatical gives to a congregation is apparent. What
kind of spiritual food does a congregation want?

There are many things we need to consider for our health and our
churches. Sabbaticals aren't the only change that needs to be made. We
should be incorporating spiritual disciplines, Sabbath, vacation, and fun
in our lives. The health of the church depends on it.

The reason people suffer through and don't risk asking for what they need is that duty, responsibility, and expectations speak louder than health, freedom, grace, and trust.

Grace is a large part of a sabbatical. If we believe that we rely entirely on Jesus for everything, then we must live out the belief that we don't have to do everything. Yet so many pastors and spouses look at their church, their staff, and the faith of all those in their congregation and presume that it would all fall apart without them. We can be so arrogant, can't we?

Jesus invited his disciples to a time of rest.

Mark 6:31 (NIV)

Then, because so many people were coming and going that they did not even have a chance to eat, he said to them, "Come with me by yourselves to a quiet place and get some rest."

Quiet Place.

Rest.

Doesn't that sound nice?

Chapter 2

Do you Need a Sabbatical?

My Story

My sabbatical started with a substantial amount of frustration, some fatigue, and considerable bitterness, which was all mixed in a depth of sadness.

16.5 years of church ministry. 16.7 years of marriage. 3 years of graduate school. 4 cross-country moves. 4 churches.

The 4 years before my sabbatical had been extremely challenging. I was exhausted all the way around: emotionally, spiritually, physically and mentally. Although not how I would like it to have been, that is how mine began. This sabbatical wasn't because I planned it. It wasn't because someone else suggested it; but because it was essential for me to continue.

Sometimes sabbaticals are a reaction to stress.

What made it even more challenging is that my internal state was on the opposite side of the continuum from our church. Pathways Church was growing, and had just been through the fire and God was showing up. Adam, my husband, was more focused and energized than ever. At the start of 2017, our church was starting a message series titled, "Confidence is Coming Back." The challenging 4 years we had gone through as a community broke forth to a time of tremendous energy, numerical and internal growth, excitement, and exciting plans for the future. The juxtaposition to my own experience couldn't have been more striking. Because the church was in such an emotional high it made my emotional low that much more pronounced.

I felt like I was barely holding on. I kept daydreaming about a break. I fantasized about just a short amount of time where I didn't have to be the pastor's wife. Over months I thought about it and only spoke passing comments to Adam. I continued to try to power through my emptiness.

In January, after a beautiful and busy season of Thanksgiving, Christmas, and New Years; the sadness/ fatigue/ bitterness/ frustration mixture was speaking very loudly. It was trying to tell me something, and I wasn't listening, except in my daydreams, which I thought couldn't be a reality.

Like many years before, at the beginning of the New Year, I sat down to prayerfully write out what I thought God was saying to me about the upcoming year. No matter how hard I tried, I just couldn't seem to look ahead at the year. I had never experienced that before, and I knew something was wrong. I didn't hear anything from God. I was only feeling/tasting/sensing my deep discontent and what I thought was silence from God. It turns out that God was speaking. He was saying I couldn't go on without a break. No planning for the year was necessary. What was necessary was rest.

That week I took a walk in a nature preserve close to our home. It took a bitterly cold wind, the quiet of the snow-covered woods and tears that I couldn't stop to get me to hear. Maybe it took those harsh elements to wear down my near-sighted thinking.

In that isolated space, I heard God.

I realized that once again I was filtering my thoughts and choices through my husband's ministry. I felt like God said to me, "Why can't you have a break? Because Adam is a pastor? I am not limited by that, and neither are you. Take a break."

And it was settled.

All of my hesitations and fears blew away with that wintery wind.

So I called my husband and told him I was going to go on a sabbatical.

Do You Need A Sabbatical?

Really, the only words I need to ask you are,

Do you need a sabbatical?

If you listened to your heart, what would it say?

Maybe you need a break, maybe you don't; just make sure you pay attention.

We must not wait on others to take care of us. This is not our husband's, church boards', or any other person's responsibility. Our thoughts, feelings, actions are OUR responsibility.

If you need something, don't wait for others to notice. One of the deep-seated reasons we don't act on what we need is because we don't believe we are worthy of it. We don't feel like we deserve it. Many of us have been told to "SOLDIER ON!" in subtle and unsubtle ways. And many of us have been conditioned to take one for the team.

Why do we tell ourselves that our hearts desires aren't worth listening to? Why do we ignore what is happening in our souls and tell ourselves what we need or want is impossible?

Are you ignoring your soul?

It's easy to do. In fact, pastors and their families are rewarded when they DO ignore their needs.

- Do you say "yes" to all counseling requests? Well, then you are a true shepherd of the flock.
- Do you only have one day off a week? You are a sacrificial person.
- Do you spend all your Friday and Saturday nights with your junior high youth group? You value the next generation.
- Do you respond back to emails within ten seconds? You are accessible and organized.
- Do you neglect to take all your vacation days? You love your job.

Are you seeing what I am getting at? We are rewarded for not having boundaries. We get pats on the back for ignoring our souls until we find ourselves exhausted, needy, and emotionally spent.

That isn't pretty for our families or for our congregations.
It's your job to take care of yourself.

How many of us have seen pastors burn out and leave church ministry after neglecting their relationship with God, their physical health, their schedule, and their marriage?

A well-rested soul has much more of a shot at going the long haul.

If you need a rest, it is likely that very few people will notice. You are the only one who knows the state of your heart. You are the only one who knows what you need. If you don't know what you need, you probably need some space and rest to figure that out. There is a spiritual and emotional drain in ministry that, when unnoticed or unattended, can be dangerous to all you hold dear.

Rest isn't a luxury given to those who earn it.

Rest isn't the reward for "The Best Pastor's Wife of the Year."

Others may not understand. Really, we shouldn't need others to understand. A sabbatical, or even taking care of one's self may be perceived as selfish, but your health is worth it. Sometimes it is a struggle to define your life. Allow yourself the room to do things the way you feel is best. And when that space is not granted by others, it may take some struggle to find the freedom you need.

During my break, I was listening to Shauna Niequist being interviewed in a podcast. She was sharing about her decision to step back from church ministry for a time.

She said,

"I would never say that I have ever been particularly brave. I can say that I have been desperate. Desperation makes you brave."

Shauna took drastic measures because she was in need of rest.

Desperate rest.

People enter into sabbaticals from deliberate planning or desperation.

I hope that in the years to come that deliberate planning outweighs desperation. In whichever circumstance you find yourself, know that you are loved and that it is okay to be human. Being human means that we have times and moments of weakness, neediness, and weariness.

Isn't that a funny thought? That it is okay to be human? But if you are in ministry, you are aware that you are tempted to believe the lie that you aren't allowed to be human, or that you should be able to rise above your humanity.

Are you comfortable being human? Weak? Are you aware and at peace with the fact that sometimes you need something and have to ask for it?

If you are reading this and you find yourself thinking something like "I am pretty good right now, actually." I am so happy for you. For those of you that are doing well, here are some rhythms and practices that might be helpful to incorporate into your life to prevent burnout in the future:

- Sabbath
- Vacations or mini-vacations that involve turning off your phone, email, and social media
- Increasingly deep relationships with trusted souls
- Periodic spiritual direction or therapy
- Self- care: exercise, healthy diet, quality sleep
- Regular evaluation of your schedule and commitments
- Continued growth plans for all areas of your life: relational, spiritual, physical, emotional, and vocational
- Repeated conversations with your spouse about handling the stress of ministry
- Plan fun things to do, pursue goals and dreams in your life and find joy in the everyday tasks of life.

However, maybe you find your heart resonating with some of my experience.

Here are some signs that you may need a break:

- Unable to experience pleasure with activities that you once found enjoyable
- Lack of mental focus and clarity
- Unexplained physical pain
- Feelings of bitterness, anger, and unforgiveness toward ministry and people involved
- Consistent daydreaming
- Increase in mindless activity to escape (scrolling Instagram repeatedly)
- Chronic marriage difficulties
- Feeling directionless
- Working for years and years without a break
- Something is wrong, but you don't know what it is
- Difficulty controlling your thoughts
- Unhealthy patterns that you are unable to break

I have one caution to consider when contemplating a sabbatical. There is a temptation to run when we feel danger. Our nature tells us to flee things that cause fear. Hopelessness, hurt, and feelings of powerlessness trigger us to run. If you find yourself in this place, I caution you to pause. Sabbaticals should not be based on running away from something. Sabbaticals are a journey toward God. It is crucial that sabbaticals not become an escape. We must be careful that we are not running FROM pain, relationships, confusion, and wounds; but TO the One who can heal.

The prophet Elijah ran for his life, as recorded in I Kings 19. Jezebel threatened him, and he had good reason to believe that she meant what she said. After killing all the prophets, Jezebel was coming after Elijah. I'd be afraid, too.

In Elijah's journey away from danger, God met him with food, water, and rest. And Elijah met God with his honesty and his debilitating emotional exhaustion. Elijah prayed that he might die, and then he said, "I have had enough, Lord. Take my life."

You may have never been at the point of wanting to die, but I would speculate that most of you have had a day or two or 500 that you just wanted out of ministry.
After Elijah's sincere confession, he fell asleep. Food miraculously appeared to help him in his journey. God knew that Elijah was not strong enough. With that nourishment, he traveled forty days to Mount Horeb.

After a night of rest in a dark, lonely cave in Mount Horeb, the mountain of God, God woke Elijah.

I Kings 19:9a-11 (NIV) reads,

And the word of the Lord came to him:
"What are you doing here, Elijah?"
He replied, "I have been very zealous for the Lord God Almighty. The
Israelites have rejected your covenant, torn down your altars, and put
your prophets to death with the sword. I am the only one left, and now
they are trying to kill me too."
The Lord said, "Go out and stand on the mountain in the presence of
the Lord, for the Lord is about to pass by."

I love the question that God asked Elijah.

"What are you doing here Elijah?"

His response makes me laugh. Elijah tells God that he has been
zealous for the Lord and that he is the only prophet alive, as if God
didn't know the facts.

God was asking about his soul.

Read what happens next in I Kings 19:11a-13a:

Then a great and powerful wind tore the mountains apart and shattered the rocks before the Lord, but the Lord was not in the wind. After the wind, there was an earthquake, but the Lord was not in the earthquake. After the earthquake came a fire, but the Lord was not in the fire. And after the fire came a gentle whisper. When Elijah heard it, he pulled his cloak over his face and went out and stood at the mouth of the cave. Then a voice said to him, "What are you doing here Elijah?"

Elijah didn't adequately answer His question the first time, so God asked again. Stubborn and exhausted Elijah repeated his first answer.

Elijah isn't the only one who is stubborn and exhausted, is he?

Sometimes it takes us a few times to get it, doesn't it?
God then told Elijah to go back the way he came. Elijah went all the way to Mount Horeb only to be sent back.

If you are running, make sure you are running to God. He will give you what you need, and then He will send you where you need to go.

God asked Elijah the question, *"What are you doing here?"* two times, so it may be worth our time to answer the question ourselves:

What are you doing here?

A few questions to consider:

1. Have you ignored symptoms of burnout, uncontrolled feelings, or severe stress in your relationships?

2. Does it feel like a good time for a break? Some circumstances would warrant holding off on a sabbatical. Is it a good time in the church calendar? Will your personal life allow for more time with God?

3. Have you ever had a break? Think about the timeline of your ministry life. Have you had time away from the roles and responsibilities of ministry and work? Have you taken time to reflect back, be present in the moment, and look forward to the future?

My Story

When I was talking with Adam about taking a sabbatical, I just kept thinking and saying, "I just need it. And so I am asking for it. I am not unstable, or in a bad situation or anything, I just know that I need space."

Processing the decision with my husband was one thing. Telling the staff and church was a whole other thing. When I went to the church staff meeting to share, I could feel the tension in the room. I hadn't been to a staff meeting in a long time, and I could sense that they were wondering why I was there and what we were going to say. I didn't really prepare, because my soul, mind, and heart just felt undone.

So I shared, and I cried, a lot. As I looked around at their faces, they were sympathetic, curious, and concerned. We had all been through a tough ministry season together. I told them that I was tired. I shared that being married to a pastor was hard. I tried to reassure them that Adam and I were okay. I shared with them that I just couldn't hear God.

As I said the words that I couldn't hear God, I knew that it wasn't entirely accurate, but I couldn't figure out what WAS exactly true. I needed the space to figure it out.

I could tell that it was difficult for some of them. Some of the staff would love a sabbatical. Some of the team had been through much more than I had. But the fact that I was not on staff meant more freedom. My obligation and role were that I was married to the lead pastor.

Some of the staff also felt protective of the church. Our church had been through a lot of struggles, and they were concerned that my sabbatical would signal that something was wrong with Adam's leadership and the state of the church. Some feared that it would raise concerns about my connectedness to the church, our marriage, or my stability.

For some people, what I needed didn't appear to be what was best for the church. But I am a firm believer in "what is truly good for the individual is good for the whole." Sometimes what is best for an individual shakes things up for the whole system and causes disruption and a temporary instability, but I truly believe that what God thinks is best for the individual offers something beautiful to the whole, something healthier. I was banking on that belief.

As Adam and I told the board, the staff, our family, and our friends, one of the unexpected dilemmas was whether to announce my sabbatical to the church or not. The way that I am wired, I kept thinking, "My sabbatical is not a big deal. Of course, we will tell the church. Why would we not tell them?" But my opinion was met with several people believing that I should quietly take a break. Our church's years of difficult struggles made making the decision a bit hazy.

Very real wounds from before Adam and I were at Pathways caused
mistrust and fear to be triggered very easily. It made communicating
about these things more challenging than in most church environments.
The decision was a difficult one that we battled (and I use the word
"battled" intentionally) for more than a week. Adam and I went back
and forth. We flip-flopped from one opinion to another. The decision
was discussed initially between us. We then went to a few of the
leadership staff and the board to ask for their opinion. After talking to
the board and a few staff leaders, we weren't even close to a consensus.
In fact, about half felt that it should be announced and half felt that
announcing it would be more harmful than helpful. At this point, we
were tired of trying to make the decision. It is these unseen
conversations and dilemmas that are exhausting to pastors!

At this point, I begged Adam to ask some trusted, mature, long-term
lay-leaders in our church to see what they thought. One hundred
percent of them advised that it should be announced. Every church has
its own history, ethos, and ways of communication. For our church, it
was better to err on the side of openness and communication.

Adam decided to announce in a weekend service. I didn't really like
the attention, but I have a very fervent belief that the truth is always the
best way, even if it makes things more difficult in the present.

The Sunday morning that Adam announced it, I was sitting in the front row. Adam was nervous, and it showed. His voice trembled a little bit, and it was apparent that he was uncomfortable. But as I watched him tell the congregation about me, as a person, and why I was taking a sabbatical, I have never felt more protected by him in our marriage. I felt sheltered by God. In fact, I felt a sense of peace like I have never experienced. It was as if God took every ounce of fear and uncertainty from me. It did not matter at all to me that morning how people reacted to the news. They could have been mad, scared, irritated, judgmental, curious, etc., all I felt was loved and protected.

There on the front row in front of hundreds of people staring at me, this gift of encompassing peace was God whispering to me, "I know you need this break, and I want you to be sheltered in Me. It is where I want you, Laura. Rest, even now as it is being announced. You know that some people are afraid that something is wrong, but you can rest in Me." It was one of the most supernatural moments of my life. I didn't need anyone's approval. The freedom I experienced that morning was just what I needed to launch into my sabbatical.

God wants us to have good things.

It reminds me of Matthew 7:9-11 (NIV):

Suppose your son asks for bread. Which of you will give him a stone?
Or suppose he asks for a fish. Which of you will give him a snake?
Even though you are evil, you know how to give good gifts to your
children. How much more will your Father who is in heaven give good
gifts to those who ask him!

The reactions from those around me that morning and the weeks
following were all over the map. The five main categories were: 1.
Concern, 2. Critical Questioning, 3. Silence, 4. Loving Support, and 5.
Enthusiastic Encouragement.

A lot of people at church that I talked to that day were concerned.
They had the reasonable questions of "Are you okay? Are you and
Adam okay?," and "Are you going to leave Pathways?" I could tell
when people walked up to me that they were concerned, and I
immediately reassured that I really just needed a break. I think people
appreciated me telling them that I was okay. Adam received a lot of
texts, emails, and questions also. These questions never bothered me. I
felt love and care in them. When churches experience trauma, change
and uncertainty will trigger fear responses. It is not only individuals and
families that suffer trauma. Churches, as a whole, can experience

trauma. Looking back, my sabbatical triggered a trauma response in our battle-worn church.

One of the most challenging parts of announcing the sabbatical was responding to several critical people. I heard that a few people did not agree with my sabbatical, but they never came to me. I had the choice of seeking them out or continuing on my sabbatical without talking to them. Because I had begun my sabbatical when I heard the criticism, I chose to not pursue them mostly from being too emotionally tired to pursue them. I felt that their judgment of my sabbatical was more about where they were rather than something that I needed to defend. Some people react to new ideas and unconformity because of their own rigidity and lack of empathy. I really needed the space and separateness from church, and I felt like if I had sought them out, it would jeopardize my focus.

One of the critical questions that I heard more than once was, "How can you take a sabbatical if Adam isn't taking one?" The glaring sexism of this question left me stunned every time it was asked, and unfortunately, I was asked that question quite a few times. Do you think a man would have to justify his decisions based on his wife's plans? The answer is no. There is a very unhealthy dynamic for married women that we are not considered a whole person, but only part of a marriage. What people were implying with that question was that I did not deserve, nor was it okay for me, to take a sabbatical unless my husband took one.

I had many responses to that question in my bitter daydreams, but after prayer and hearing it so many times, I calmly told them that Adam wasn't in need of one, but I was, and so it would be unnecessarily cruel to myself to wait until he needed one. I shared that I felt the freedom to take a sabbatical even though it wasn't conventional.

The second big question I was asked was, "But you don't work at the church, right?" Some people just wanted to know if I was working in the church, and others couldn't understand how a pastor's wife would need a sabbatical. The tone of voice had a lot to do with how I interpreted this question. This question comes more from a lack of understanding. I had to take a deep breath and go to my happy place when asked how I could take a sabbatical if I didn't work at the church. Since the vast majority of the readers of this book are in ministry, I think you can imagine the mild irritation that this question could cause. To be involved in unpaid ministry for decades, and then treated as if it isn't challenging, feels like a slap in the face.

For the unpaid spouse of a pastor, the ministry of the church enters our home every day. It enters my marriage in beautiful ways, but the stress divides us sometimes in destructive ways. Its beauty gives more significant meaning to my life, yet it is a burden I bear with my husband. The privilege of serving others is joined with the weariness of years of service. It is difficult sometimes when I am expected to serve out of my education and profession for free. There have been many times I felt used. I have no official responsibility or position, yet the cost is high. That is why I felt the liberty to take a break.

Over time, God helped me to let go of the fact that some people didn't understand how this paycheck-less job would be even more of a reason to take a sabbatical. I think I assumed that people would realize and have empathy that doing an unpaid role for 17 years would be challenging and tiring. Sometimes people need to be reminded. That is part of the strangeness of being in ministry. We have to explain ourselves to A LOT of people. We don't have the luxury of making decisions only for ourselves and our own family. For me, I had to explain myself to 1000 people and then be questioned for why I was tired after volunteering for years.

For people who don't feel that a break from ministry is justified, I would advise them to evaluate their beliefs about Sabbath, grace, and empathy for themselves. Chances are, they are cruel to themselves, and it comes out as judgment to others.

I know that many volunteers give, sacrifice, and offer their time and talents to the church. If those faithful servants wanted to take a 3-month break from service in the course of their lifetime, I would say to them, "May your rest be blessed."

For me, even more challenging to experience than the critical questions was the deafening silence that came from several people. I think those reactions were the most distracting to my thoughts because I didn't know what they were thinking. How I interpreted the silence was with the words, "You are being selfish. You must be pretty messed up. I have never heard of a pastor's wife taking a sabbatical. Why would you need to take a break from your church family? You must be either lazy or weak." If I were to choose, I would prefer to have heard these audible, critical questions than my own internal interpretation any day. The temptation to project what people's silence means is a genuine and deadly threat to our thought life. But we have a choice on what we focus on. Mindreading does our thought life a disservice.

I am so thankful that most of the responses were of encouragement. I got a lot of high-fives from people at church and a ton of hugs. It felt good to be blessed by those responses before my break. My small group was caring and loving, and a comfortable place to just be. And I had many friends who were supportive. Some people came up to me and told me how brave I was, or that they would love a break.

I was encouraged by several spiritual leaders in our community. I met with a spiritual director to talk about my plan on sabbatical, and when I shared with her what I was doing, she exuberantly smiled and told me that she was so happy for me and that it was wise to rest when I knew I was tired. She celebrated the scary steps with me.

Also, a few weeks into my sabbatical I visited a nearby church. When I told the pastor who I was and why I was visiting, he met me with a hearty hug and an energetic, "Wow! Way to go!"

This is the chapter that I wish I had been able to read BEFORE I went on sabbatical. Of all the aspects of my sabbatical, I definitely wish I could re-do the communicating portion of this time.

Looking back, I was so unprepared to communicate about my sabbatical to my husband, the staff, my friends, the church, and even people outside of the church. I think because I was feeling directionless myself, and still trying to understand what God was doing in me, my inner confusion was very apparent in the way I communicated with others.

There were several things we learned that I hope will help some of you.

First of all, I was a mess when we went to tell the staff. I think this led to worry and uncertainty. I wish I had given more thought about what I would say when we told the team. They also were unclear about how to respond and communicate with me because I didn't express what I wanted from them. What I wanted was a little communication, encouragement, and care, but they didn't know what to do because I didn't ask for what I wanted. I wish I had asked for them to check in with me if they had questions or concerns.

Secondly, I wish I had been more involved in my husband's writing of the announcement. I was so ready to be on sabbatical at that time that I just wanted it done, and it was communicated a little differently than if I had been involved in the wording of the announcement.

Many times what we desperately need is on the other side of difficult circumstances and challenging situations. Those challenging circumstances are what keep us stagnant and afraid. One of the challenging aspects of communicating about a sabbatical is that one who is entering sabbatical is probably in a place of needing to focus inwardly. But of course, the demands of talking about something so potentially vulnerable during a time of weariness leaves an opening for miscommunication, fear, confusion, and gossip.

Thinking through the communication of the sabbatical is well worth the effort. The potential negative outcomes of a poorly handled entry into sabbatical are great. Although there is unease and probably many opinions about how to communicate this, it is worth the time spent.

Here are a few things to consider:

1.   Think about the concentric circles of your life and communicate in order of those closest to you personally and in the church. Start with your family, then move to closest friends, then the board and staff, and then your wider community. Those who are closest to you should know more and be your first priority.

2.   Think about what you will call your time away. Will it be a break? Sabbatical? Study break? Every church culture, region, and situation is different. Have very clear communication about how you, your spouse, and the staff are talking about it. This will reduce confusion.

3.   Bring trusted advisors in to help you with the decisions of details about your sabbatical and the communication process.

4.   Help others know what you need and want.

5.   Send an update mid-sabbatical. I didn't do this, and I wish that I had.

6.   Have a laid out timeline, but leave room for flexibility.

7.   Leave a little bit of time for people to say "goodbye" and ask their questions, and to reassure people of what is happening.

8.   Be honest. This does not mean that you need to tell everything, but do not in anyway say anything that does not represent who you are and what God is leading you to.

9.   The announcement and communication of your sabbatical will depend on many factors, including: your role, church size, established way of communicating, and ministry involvements.

10.   Deal with negativity before your sabbatical if at all possible, especially with those you are close to. If someone appears to be displeased, I recommend dealing with it head-on. Talk it out before you leave so that you don't have to think about it during your time. Going right into the discomfort will allow you to enter into your sabbatical with courage.

Chapter 4

Sabbatical Preparation

My Story

Of all the different aspects, preparing for sabbatical was the easiest for me. I had more dreams and imaginations about my time away than could have been accomplished. My temptation was to have too many ideas.

In my view, there are two different aspects of preparation for a sabbatical. First, there is the "nuts and bolts" preparation. Secondly, there is the heart and mind preparation for the actual sabbatical time. Neither should be neglected.

For me, the "nuts and bolts" preparation was more challenging. This included trying to figure out how long it should be and what my boundaries would be. My preparation time was only a few weeks, and much of that time was spent on how to communicate it to other people, reassuring them that I was okay, and very little time was actually spent on the preparation for how I would spend the time.

Space, rest, and healing were so inviting, that for me, I knew that I could quickly create a plan for how to spend my sabbatical. I approached my prayer time with God with the focus on what I should put in my plan. What I didn't think about (although now it seems like a "duh") was that it was God's plan all along. I really didn't know where

He would lead, what He would teach me, or what wounds I would go back to for healing. The preparation was less about my plan and more about putting my heart and mind in a place of being led.

I cannot emphasize enough how important boundaries are. They are so easy to talk about and so tricky to implement, but when you go into your sabbatical knowing what you want, you have done half of the hard work.

I found the internal boundaries of my thoughts the most difficult to guard initially. I spent the first couple of weeks trying to shake a few hurtful comments from my thought life. As I eased into the time and space, I found it so peaceful to rest, be present, and get excited about how I would spend the time.

My sabbatical included not attending my church, but visiting other churches in my area. By their choice, my children continued to go to our church, and they didn't seem to have any worries or difficulties with my being on sabbatical. In fact, they joined in helping my husband give me space for additional reading and prayer time. They were a precious gift to me.

If I had had more time to plan, I would have tried to take a sabbatical that was entirely away from work. I was still homeschooling one of our daughters, but the flexibility of this provided me ample space for prayer and study. But because I was still homeschooling, I had to be even more purposeful with my boundaries so that I could live out my sabbatical the way that I envisioned.

My children knew that I was tired. I wanted to be a healthy model to them. I felt that my sabbatical modeled self and marriage care to them. It taught them that they are not the only members of the family who have needs.

I continued to do a few things with friends. I went to book club. I continued to meet with our small group that I love. But I only did activities that I wanted to do. Call me over-spiritual, but I invited God into every commitment. I knew that I would get too busy if I didn't let Him in the planning of my calendar.

One of the things I did not anticipate was the number of people from church who wanted to have coffee with me, meet with me, and spend time with me when they learned of my sabbatical. Honestly, I got more requests right before my sabbatical than I had in the last 4 years combined. It left me feeling pulled in two directions. I wanted to be kind, but I did not have the time to meet with people. And because of the number of requests, I sensed that it was more out of concern. For me, I tried to discern each request, and I asked myself a few questions as I considered each invitation. Did I need to reassure them over email and set the boundary that I couldn't meet with them right now? Was this person already close enough to me that I did want to meet with them?

It may have been perceived as distant, but I chose to say "no" to many of the requests. With my sabbatical so close, I didn't want to spend weeks leading up to it taking care of others at the neglect of my family. I was tired, and I just didn't feel like I could do it all. I let myself be human.

Because I had been advised to have very set parameters, I borrowed the phrase, "I was advised to...," a few times when my boundaries were questioned. And now you can use that phrase when you need to because I am advising you to know, communicate, and keep your boundaries!

The boundaries of what things Adam and I discussed were much more ongoing and challenging. Adam and I decided to not talk about ANYTHING church-related unless there was an emergency or crucial information I needed to know about. This was challenging because significant things were happening at church. The church was growing, and Adam and the team were in the middle of planning a significant building expansion. I wasn't involved in ANYTHING. Ministry spaces, rooms, design, ideas... I had no idea what was happening.

Not talking about church was as challenging as you can imagine. But it was a gift in several ways. First, we realized that we had talked about church WAY too much and we found ourselves looking at each other with little to say. It forced us to connect outside of the topic of ministry. This wasn't fun at all, actually. It was painful because it uncovered deeper wounds in our marriage that our ministry distractions were covering. We realized that we had been distracting ourselves by talking too much about church life. And we realized how much my unlived dreams were affecting our connection.

Looking back, I wonder if that unattended wound was the real reason I was led into sabbatical. Yes, I was tired, but that was only the symptom of the much broader problem.

Adam later shared with me that not talking about church was a weight lifted from him. For those months he didn't have to make decisions about what to share with me and what information to withhold. We all know that is a delicate balance. Adam also shared that he found a greater degree of empathy and understanding for pastors' spouses. I was able to find language and space to share my thoughts, and the space helped him to listen.

People in your life may need to be reminded of your boundaries. That's okay. People forget. Sometimes I had to remind Adam of what

I needed. Near the end of my sabbatical, Adam was very upset about something that happened at church. I was in the basement on the treadmill, and he came down venting, sharing a situation with me as he was angrily lifting weights. Because I was only a week or two away from entering back into church life, I thought, "I will let him talk. He is my husband, and he wants to talk to his wife. I will listen, support, and give it to God. No advice. And I won't hold on to it." I really wanted to funnel it to God, and I wanted to be there for him, but I realized after a few minutes that my shoulders were becoming tense, and I was feeling frustrated. So I had a choice of whether to stop the conversation or let him continue. After a few minutes, I asked him if he could find another person to talk to about it. And he lovingly lifted weights in silence.

I relished the two and a half months away. I didn't want to waste it on a "yes" that I didn't really want to give. And when I entered back into congregational life, my "yeses" were more purposeful and full of the kind of ministry I wanted to do. This is challenging work, though. But it is worth it. Hard work bears fruit, and it makes us stronger.

Preparing for a Sabbatical

I write my story from my perspective. My husband has been a staff spouse for most of our married life until he became a lead pastor couple of years ago. Some of the logistics may be different when it comes to how your sabbatical will look and how it is communicated, but the principles are the same.

The stressful effects of ministry are not only for those in senior leadership. In fact, it can be quite the opposite. The stress of a young marriage, young family, inexperience in leadership, schedule of ministry, and college debt are even more of a reason to take a short break.

If your church or situation doesn't allow for a sabbatical, I suggest being creative with your rest. Perhaps you could step back from volunteering for a short time while continuing to attend services.

If you have young children still at home, taking intentional rest is more challenging, yet may be more important. If you are drowning in ministry, don't wait to make changes.

Set a Vision for your Sabbatical

Intentionality and purpose are essential for a sabbatical. God has in mind what He would like for you. When we pray, with a focus on silence, we are more able to listen to what He wants for us. The more we can connect with God as we set the vision for the sabbatical, the more we can set boundaries, make a plan, stick to it, and feel a sense of peace about how we are spending the time.

Although God may completely turn your vision and plan upside down, it is still good to have a direction you are going. The key is to be open to the Spirit as God changes our path.

Your purpose and vision for your sabbatical will most likely correlate with your most significant needs. Having an area of focus or two can help you determine if something is worth your time. If you want to focus on reducing your anxiety, it probably isn't the best decision to take an online course on how to be more productive.

As you think about how to spend your time, think about taking some trips or retreats. Are there ways you can get out of your usual surroundings? Marking your time with a few retreats, even if they are short trips, can make a difference in hearing the Lord. If we want to see new things spiritually, being in a different environment can be helpful. God wants to take our hearts and minds to new places. New physical locations often spur new thinking, creativity, and the feeling of being more alive.

Start with Rest

One of my mentors and the author of *Anonymous*, and *Ready, Set Rest*, Alicia Britt Chole, suggests starting off a prayer retreat with a nap. A nap was not what I was expecting her to say, but nevertheless, with every retreat I take, I think of those wise words. If I am not sleepy, I rest or take a slow walk outside.

When we rest right from the beginning, several things happen. First, it gives us strength for what comes next. Secondly, it puts us in the proper place. God is the one who does the work. God is the one who leads.

Planned rest (as in "put in on the calendar ahead of time") is a good idea for a sabbatical. Look through the calendar and schedule it. If it needs to be adjusted, then you can be flexible.

Your sabbatical should have the flavor and the beauty of how God made you. You are exquisitely made, and your experience should take on your unique personality and longings. Give some time before or at the beginning of your sabbatical to write down a list of things you love or wish to do in your time. For me, one of the things I longed for was to enjoy art. The simple act of both enjoying others art and making my own, which is very amateur, I assure you, helped settle my soul. It took me to a place where my heart was more still, where I was able to more readily notice the activity of God, my own heart, and those around me. Whether it is art, music, nature, or other interests, make sure to include beauty in your sabbatical.

Sabbatical is a unique time where we can pursue God and experience and submit our hearts to Him. It may be a good idea to get a book on spiritual disciplines. You can take some time to experience God in different traditions than you are accustomed to. This fresh insight can create pathways and experiences that lead to renewal and spiritual insight. While the purpose of a sabbatical is ministry rest, the activity of sabbatical is a pursuit of God. The absence of ministry to others gives us space to renew the attention and focus on the One our heart needs and the Love that captures us.

Create a Plan

One thing to consider is what books, resources, Scripture, etc., to include in your sabbatical. I would say to have a list to start with, and as the Lord leads, be flexible. You will probably accomplish less than you think you will. Let that be okay. Resist the urge to be productive and check off "to-do's" in your sabbatical.

One fundamental way to honor God in your sabbatical is to take care of your body. Have you been ignoring an injury? Have you been curious about that new class at the YMCA? Is your dog begging to go for a walk with you? Honor God when you sleep, when you eat, and when you move.

Creating Heart Space: Surrender in Sabbatical

Sabbaticals are really about letting go. This letting go is relinquishing control of productivity, reputation, influence, work, affirmation, and ego. Giving up those things is like a parent prying a toy from the hands of a toddler at a toy store. It ain't pretty. And it involves tantrums and gawkers.

One lesson from Sabbath and sabbatical is that we learn that we are not indispensable. Things still run without you, and that is good!

But sabbatical can be so much more than letting go of the work, or the position, or the influence. Sabbatical can lead an individual to a place where we surrender attachments to things, people, and ideas. Attachments form so quietly. We need space and perspective to see the attachments that have developed. Once they are acknowledged, they can be surrendered at the cross of Christ.

If we spend our sabbatical controlling how it will go, trying to attain knowledge or skills, and anxiously try to pack a million items on our to-do list, we are missing the point. Sabbatical reminds us that more isn't always better.

If there is one thing you can focus on in the sabbatical preparation phase, it is to have a surrendered heart.

As I was preparing to write this morning, I was using my tea kettle to heat up some water for a cup of tea, and I wondered how long it has been since I totally emptied out the water in the kettle to clean it properly. Stagnant water is a bacteria factory. Sabbatical is the emptying of the stagnant water of our lives. Let God lead the filling back up phase. He will do a much better job than we could ever hope to accomplish.

I imagine that God will take your heart on a journey that you cannot anticipate. Trust Him. Let Him lead. He is a much better navigator than we will ever be.

Creating a Sabbatical Team

As you think about how you want your sabbatical to look, one important consideration is with whom you want and need interaction. If you are in a small group, would interacting with them be beneficial, or would you be tempted to lead and give more than what God would want for you at this time? What friends do you want to spend time with? Do you have a therapist, mentor, or spiritual director you want to meet with, or should you find one before you enter sabbatical?

The people that you spend your time with will significantly affect your sabbatical. Give it thought and prayer and choose wisely. If a person is draining, then you have your answer. And if you need to make a change mid-way through it, be courageous enough to communicate that.

There is a temptation to try to do too many things and meet with too many people on sabbatical. Err on the side of simplicity. You can always add, but it is more difficult to take away.

It may be helpful to have a close spiritual friend to whom you can be accountable. This could include updating this friend on how you are doing, what you are doing, challenges you are facing, and ways they can be praying for you.

There is an unhealthy reality for many pastors. Pastors rarely spiritually submit to others. They may submit vocationally to a board or to their boss at work. They spiritually speak into many lives week by week, yet who is speaking into their life? I'm not talking about the pastors you watch online or the podcasts you subscribe to. Who is that up-close person who is telling you the truth? Who is challenging you to take a fierce look in the mirror of your soul? Pastors spend their lives guiding and shepherding others, but they rarely submit to others for direction and correction.

That is dangerous.

A mentor or spiritual director from outside of your church body may be helpful to you. Spiritual direction is time spent together focusing on the activity of God in a directee's life. Spiritual direction has many things to offer someone on sabbatical. Its emphasis on our relationship to God, the quiet tempo, and prayerfulness of spiritual direction is ideal for sabbaticals. It can be beneficial to process with a spiritual director how God is moving. Sabbatical can be a wilderness, and a spiritual director can be a friend along the way. You can find more information on spiritual direction and sabbatical support programs through "*Tree by Water.*" Information can be found in the back of this book.

Boundaries on Sabbatical

Ah, boundaries.

Everyone says they are useful and essential and beautiful until the hard work needs to be done. If you have never read the book, *Boundaries: When to Say Yes, How to Say No, How to Take Control of Your Life* by Henry Cloud and John Townsend, stop right now and order the book or the whole series. I believe everyone in the world should read that book.

Don't make the mistake of thinking about your boundaries AFTER they are trounced on. Be proactive with thinking about the different areas of your life.

Regardless of whether your spouse is on a sabbatical at the same time or not, talking about your boundaries is essential. There are many things to consider. What topics would be off limits during the sabbatical? What boundaries do you need aside from church life? Do you need more time alone than usual? Do you need more date nights?

If you are going on sabbatical together, I think it would be a great idea to get a pastor, therapist, or mentor to help you sort through these things. You may require very different things, and having someone else help you in the creation of a plan could help reduce conflict or the possibility of unspoken and unmet needs.

If you have children, particularly at home, it is wise to think about how your sabbatical will affect them. Assuming they are old enough to understand the difference in your schedule, share your heart with them. You can even tell them what you need from them and how it will affect them. Ask them what they need. Think about how their life will be different. Perhaps they want to join you, or maybe they really do not want to be away from church for that long. Do you need to be less involved in their school and sports during sabbatical? Do you want to find people to help with childcare to allow you more time for reflection, retreat, or reading?

You may want to change the time and involvement with friends and different groups that you normally spend time with. It is crucial not only to communicate about your sabbatical but also to consider stepping back from commitments. There may be friends you see more or less of during your sabbatical.

My friend Teresa became my "sabbatical accountability" friend. She is a friend I confided in and sought accountability from before my sabbatical. Her feedback, empathy, and understanding were a gift to me. We met a few times during my sabbatical, but what was so helpful was when she would text me to check in on me. She would send me encouragement, and I could text her about how I was spending my time and what was happening in my heart.

My suggestion is to spend time with people that you see in your "normal" life. But don't spend time with people who drain you or only want something from you. It may sound cliché, but pray when you are asked to do something or be somewhere. Filter the decision through the question, "Will this fill me in my sabbatical time or drain me?" We all know that certain people and circumstances can drain us for a day or two. To say "yes" to an engagement that drains you is to be disobedient as a steward of the sabbatical.

It is important to think about what you really want on your sabbatical and to stick to your guns. Whatever you do, there will be people who disapprove. There will almost certainly be someone who is hurt by your boundaries. But you are not responsible for other people's feelings. You are responsible for being loving, kind, truthful, and faithful to God. When you are on sabbatical, I recommend being very persistent in saying "no" to any church engagement, even on Facebook, Instagram or other social media platforms unless there is a serious emergency. And if that happens, enter swiftly back into your sabbatical once you are able.

If you remain in ministry for your entire life, this sabbatical is a brief and beautiful time. If you fail to set and keep your boundaries, you are wasting this precious gift.

Steward it well, friend. Say the very difficult "no."

Questions to Consider:

1. Is there anything in my life that I need to STOP doing (Netflix, certain activities and appointments, etc.)?

2. What passions or beauty do I need to include?

3. What can I do to let go of my need for control in this sabbatical?

4. What kind of rest would be valuable to my soul?

5. What are the things that I can let go of to be more open to the love and presence of God?

6. How can I take care of my body?

7. Who would be life-giving to me on my sabbatical? Who would NOT be life-giving?

8.   What boundaries am I going to set?

9.   Who do I want to be on my sabbatical team (spiritual director, accountability friend, etc.)?

10.   What boundaries am I going to set? With my husband? Friends? Church? Family? In my mind?

11.   How many retreats do you want to do? Where? When? (Get them on the calendar!)

12.   What books do you want to read? What is your soul needing?

13.   What books of Scripture do you feel led to read? Do you want to read Scripture in small portions or in large, overarching ways?

14.   Is there something you feel led to do that you are resisting?

15.   What things will you eliminate to create space?

Chapter 5

Sabbatical As A Pilgrimage

Before you enter this chapter, will you read Psalm 23 out loud, slowly? We often rush through the familiar. Breathe. Slow your mind. Psalm 23 has much to say to our souls in the pilgrimage of sabbatical.

Psalm 23 (NIV)

A Psalm of David.
The Lord is my shepherd, I lack nothing.
He makes me lie down in green pastures,
he leads me beside quiet waters, he refreshes my soul.
He guides me along the right paths for his name's sake.
Even though I walk through the darkest valley,
I will fear no evil for you are with me; your rod and your staff,
they comfort me. You prepare a table before me in the
presence of my enemies. You anoint my head with oil;
my cup overflows. Surely your goodness and love
will follow me all the days of my life,
and I will dwell in the house of the Lord forever.

What a beautiful psalm for sabbatical!

Psalm 23 has a message for us. Above all of the comforting language, it is a psalm about a shepherding God leading His beloved.

Our life and faith are communal in so many ways. Our faith is not only our own. We start our first 18 years (at least) in family. We have celebrations with friends. We are mentored by others. We worship in congregations of like-minded and life-hearted people. We feel safety in small groups. We reach out to others when we are in need. And our loving embrace is open for others.

And yet, there is solitude in our faith that is to be embraced in sabbatical. Sabbatical is mostly a solo endeavor. No one else can fully understand the pilgrimage that the Lord will lead you on. In our age of over-sharing on social media, sabbatical has a sacredness that is best enjoyed in the deepest parts of our soul.

Psalm 23 is a psalm that we share together to speak of our individual journey with the Lord.

My Story

In the first few weeks of sabbatical, I felt as if a load had been lifted. I felt like myself again, and a strange thing happened. The depression that I realized was a guest in my soul was suddenly sent packing.

I did not know that I had been depressed until I wasn't.
When I voiced my need to have a break and set my course to be closer
to God, more connected to myself, and to figure out what I really
wanted to do with my life, the fog around me dissipated. Before, I was
in a haze. I was reasonably good at doing what "made sense." I could
fill the role of pastor's wife, wife, and mother, and all the while I was
ignoring my heart. Once I was listening to my heart and to my God, I
felt reborn. My body felt lighter and moved smoothly. My heart
connected with the people around me. Adam also noticed, mentioning
early on that I carried myself with more confidence than ever.

One remarkable gift that I felt was God's enormous patience with me. I
really had no idea what God was doing in my heart, but I felt so
comforted that I didn't need to know. I remember telling people, "I
don't know what God wants me to do, but that is okay."

One aspect of a physical pilgrimage is that it is a journey to a new
space. I visited a different church every week in my sabbatical. Our
area has a significant Catholic and Lutheran presence, and I wanted to
participate in different denominations and styles of worship than what I
was used to.

One of the first churches I attended was a well-respected Lutheran
church just down the street from my home. I know the pastor's wife

from a local homeschooling group. She is a woman I had come to respect deeply, so I thought I would start there.

At one point in the service, everyone started greeting one another. I looked down at the order of service, and it said there was a portion of time dedicated to "passing the peace." Ummm. What??? Pass the peace??? I thought, "Stay cool, Laura. Okay, I can be peaceful, and I can pass that along. Laura, you've got this!" So I turned around, and I said, "Hello, how are you tonight?" To which they replied, "Peace be with you."

I turned to the person across the aisle and smiled as if I knew what I was doing and I said, "Hello, how are you?" They replied, "Peace be with you."

Oh, Laura, you are such a dork sometimes! So for all of you who have never "passed the peace," what you need to do is say to your pew neighbors, "Peace be with you."

I almost started laughing out loud at myself.

I then had to whisper to an usher as to the theological beliefs of whether I could take communion at the altar. It was a little bit humbling to be a newbie to a church.

My experience that night gave me a greater appreciation of the anxiety of attending a church for the first time. After the service, I am sure everyone in attendance knew I was new to their church and they absolutely knew that I wasn't Lutheran!

Sabbaticals, like pilgrimages, take a big step of courage. It definitely took a big step of courage for me to take a break. We can be comforted with the fact that we don't have to lead our crazy jumbled life. It is the Lord who leads. The Lord is my shepherd, and He is a perfect Shepherd.

Stages of Sabbatical

I really love metaphors that involve journeys, and as boring as my kids think I am, I love an adventure, well, an adventure that isn't too dangerous, anyway. I love visiting new places, and I love hiking and being outside, so the concept of pilgrimage resonates with me.
A pilgrimage is a journey to a sacred place to be obedient and closer to the Lord. It is an act of religious devotion. A pilgrimage takes time. A pilgrimage means leaving the familiar and the routine.

I have never taken a physical pilgrimage to a sacred place, yet my sabbatical was an internal spiritual pilgrimage that led me to a more authentic place in my soul and closeness with God. That is a quest He invites us to over and over.

The metaphor of pilgrimage resonates for sabbaticals because our faith is an adventure, and adventures involve risk and exploration. There are common themes that emerge when looking at your journey.

The Preparation

In Chapter 4 we took a look at preparing for your sabbatical. Dismissing the importance of preparation can be as dangerous as trying to go on a vacation without knowing your destination, how you will get there, and the supplies you will need.

There is a funny thing that God usually does with our preparation. He loves to surprise us. We prayerfully prepare, but we cannot plan what God will have for us. Our preparation should be focused on opening space in our hearts, minds, and time for God's all-knowing lead.

Starting Out on the Journey

Psalm 23: 1-3a

The Lord is my shepherd, I lack nothing.
He makes me lie down in green pastures,
he leads me beside quiet waters, he refreshes my soul.

The best place to start is surrendering it all to Jesus. It's tempting to start off at high speed. Start slow. Start with rest. Being very intentional about the initial pace on sabbatical will help you to be intentional on your entire journey. Because rest is a primary purpose, it will take intention, boundaries, and determination to be focused on rest in the beginning.

Some of you will collapse and have no problem at all sleeping, getting a massage, or scheduling coffee with a friend. For you, this will be easy. For some of you, it will feel like torture. You will look around and feel the (almost) uncontrollable urge to clean and organize every closet. Do things that you enjoy doing. Enjoy simple pleasures like having a cup of tea in the afternoon. Make a nice meal. Savor each bite. Light a candle and watch the flame for a couple minutes.

One common difficulty when we have space and solitude is that we become **VERY** aware of our thoughts, and I am not referring to the nice thoughts.

When we increase silence and decrease busy activity, it leaves us with the awareness of the thoughts in our heads. When we enter solitude and silence, it is scary how many insecurities, fears, bitterness, anger, loneliness, and impure thoughts emerge that we didn't know were there. They were there all along. We just put ourselves in environments that were louder.

We have many defense mechanisms to protect our fragile thoughts. But on sabbatical, knowledge of our thoughts is often a critical first step. Dealing with those destructive thoughts first thing is essential. Our thoughts have power over us. They give us energy or suck us dry.

Walk slowly in the beginning. I mean that literally. Move slowly. Move with much intention. Think with much purpose. Make every choice with intention. This can be a time of gaining more control and intentionality over one's life. This is important for everyone, but especially for those in ministry, where control over one's life slips slowly into others hands with each "yes," and "sure, I will do that."

There is a temptation in ministry to lose your identity to others'
expectations. As Christ followers we are asked to give our lives, not our
identities. Jesus was the perfect picture of this. He gave everything, but
not WHO he was. He never gave his essence away, and we should
follow His example. When we say "yes" to things we don't want to, we
are giving our identity and freedom away.

Walking the Journey

Psalm 23:3b-5a

He guides me along the right paths for his name's sake.
Even though I walk through the darkest valley,
I will fear no evil, for you are with me; your rod and your staff,
they comfort me. You prepare a table before me
in the presence of my enemies.

The journey isn't all green pastures and quiet waters. That is a huge
bummer. His "right paths" in verse 3 lead us to "the darkest valley" in
verse 4, and the valley is a difficult place. Without a doubt, it is a place
we would choose to journey around. We would much rather trek
easier routes, but the darkest valleys are essential to the journey of
sabbatical, and they are essential for our souls.

You could have some ideas to get through the valley faster and easier, but what I have found is that God is the leader of the valleys, and he doesn't deviate from his plan because you have a better route.

You might as well stop asking Him, "Are we there yet?"

The valleys of pilgrimage are the place where God deals with the shadow side of our souls. God uses the valley to draw us closer to Himself and closer to our most genuine self. He leads us there, but it is rarely fun.

Many times we think we know what we need or what the exact problem is. But if we were capable of healing ourselves, we would have done it already. The valley is the difficult place to which we are led because it is where our hearts are lovingly exposed.

Don't try to predict or prescribe what God will do in your heart. Just be open and surrendered. Leave enough room for God to surprise you. Sabbatical is an ideal time where in-grained habits, addictions, cognitive patterns, and deep hurts can be examined and explored thoroughly. When we are in our regular patterns of busyness, we manage to suppress ideas of change, and we minimize problems in our life. We end up putting ourselves in environments too "noisy" to hear the Holy Spirit whispering.

As painful as losing control feels, only God can do this work. Only God can lead us to the place where our soul finds deep peace, profound healing, or supernatural courage. We are incapable of leading ourselves through this place. Spiritual directors, pastors, and therapists can walk with us, but they have only the role of pointing out what God may be leading. I hope that we in these helping professions can help people discern when and where God is leading, but it is God who does the work. God is the leader and the healer.

The valley is commonly an intense and vulnerable time of a sabbatical. This is usually the phase where spiritual, emotional, and psychological bondage can be broken. The promise of this hard work could lead you to places of greater freedom, joy, and peace.

Don't rush.

God will just take you around the mountain to pass through the valley a second time. Has anyone else been there?

Conclusion and Celebration

Psalm 23:5b- 5

You anoint my head with oil; my cup overflows.
Surely your goodness and love will follow me
all the days of my life,
and I will dwell in the house of the Lord forever.

Endings are important. The way in which we finish a sabbatical has implications for how we process the entire journey and how we re-enter back into congregational life.

Ending your sabbatical with a ritual, such as a nice dinner with those close to you, or a prayer retreat, or a blessing are examples of formally signaling the end of the sabbatical. Don't be so quick to enter back into your "normal" life that you neglect the conclusion. Take time to celebrate.

One of the ways you could celebrate would be to spend time looking over your journal. Consider writing out in a list form the things that God showed you during your time. Doing this helps seal the treasured moments forever.

Before we go into the process questions, it may be wise to read Psalm 23 one more time. Read it slowly. Read it aloud. Let every word sink in deeper.

Psalm 23

A Psalm of David.

The Lord is my shepherd, I lack nothing.
He makes me lie down in green pastures,
he leads me beside quiet waters, he refreshes my soul.
He guides me along the right paths or his name's sake.
Even though I walk through the darkest valley,
I will fear no evil for you are with me; your rod and your staff,
they comfort me. You prepare a table before me in the
presence of my enemies. You anoint my head with oil;
my cup overflows. Surely your goodness and love
will follow me all the days of my life,
and I will dwell in the house of the Lord forever.

Questions To Consider

The Beginning

- What are your fears and joys about sabbatical?
- What do you long for in this time?

The Valley

- What lies from the enemy are you realizing?
- Do you have people to forgive?
- Do you have anyone you need to reconcile with?
- Are there patterns in your marriage or other relationships that you need to address?
- What/Who are the enemies that God is asking you to acknowledge?
- What difficulties and wounds need healing?
- What defenses have you built up to protect yourself?
- What have you been avoiding that God wants you to address?

Conclusion and Celebration

- How can you celebrate and seal your sabbatical?
- How are you different from before your sabbatical?

- What did God show you?
- What do you want to do differently when you return?
- What were the greatest gifts to be grateful for?

Chapter 6

Returning Well

My Story

The reason I thought of "Returning Well" as a chapter is because my return was clumsy. I didn't want attention drawn to myself, and when I returned on Easter Sunday, it didn't seem appropriate to mention from the platform that I had returned.

Instead of my husband sharing that I was back, I had people asking me, "So, are you back?" and others avoiding me out of fear of what to say.

Because my return wasn't announced or talked about, I think people thought they couldn't talk to me about it. I was happy to be back, but people acted a little afraid of me. It was not a very fluid return. But luckily my awkward muscle has grown over the years, and I managed just fine. I just don't think it served our people as well as it could have.

I learned so much about God and myself in the time of my sabbatical, and I wanted to come back to our congregation in a more authentic way. I didn't want our church to have a pastor's wife who wasn't living out her calling. I didn't want our congregation to have a pastor and wife with a wedge between them. All the freedom and joy that I want for myself I wish for everyone in our congregation.

Returning Well

Re-integrating into your church community takes some time and attention. It is essential for your relationships with others. People may not know how to talk to you about your sabbatical, so consider what you want to share with people before you get back. Being honest and open about your time away and what it meant for you will help you re-engage with your community.

First, consider how you want to re-engage. Do you feel it is manageable to jump right into the relationships and ministries you were involved in, or do you need to move in slowly? The answer to this question will depend much on your level of involvement, and ultimately, what you feel led to do. I would suggest entering back into relationships first, and then the roles and responsibilities second. Establishing the connection with people in your church is very important in the reengagement period.

Secondly, think about how your sabbatical can bless others. One woman came up to me before I entered sabbatical and said, "Laura, this isn't just for you. It is for us, and you will come back and have something for us." And I did. God gave me a word that I spoke to our women a few months after I returned. I think it was her words that helped me to see that I should come back open to giving, open to sharing some of the beauty that God allowed me to experience.

The gifts that we receive are not to be hoarded. They are to be experienced and then shared. Sabbatical is a time of receiving, and when we as believers receive, it often means that there is someone in need of that which we have been given.

As you go back to your congregation and to your normal pace of life, take what God has shown you and experience the beauty of your rest with those who you have the privilege to serve.

Chapter 7

After the Sabbatical

My story

I felt like the essence of my sabbatical lingered for much longer than my actual break. I continue to experience the rest and settledness over a year later. And it was months after I returned that I was still searching God's heart about what to do vocationally.

What came of the space was my realization that I did not want to spend another day missing my purpose in life. For years, since we started dating, I had allowed Adam's ministry and calling to overtake my priorities, time, and energy and I wanted my sabbatical to be a "reset." I had sabotaged what I felt that God wanted me to do over and over and over for Adam's ministry. The space of my sabbatical was a turning point.

I told Adam at the beginning of my sabbatical, "I just need a break from being a pastor's wife." Now I know that I was putting my role of being a pastor's wife over what God was asking me to do. Throughout the years I made decision after decision that I thought supported Adam, but really, I was doing damage to our marriage.

I was a co-dependent pastor's wife. That's one of the fun lessons I learned on sabbatical.

There was also a significant birth that emerged. It was from the space of sabbatical that I grew the courage to lead Tree by Water, a ministry to help people be rooted in God and true to themselves.

At the end of my sabbatical, it brought me so much joy to look at what I journaled during my sabbatical. It was a meaningful way of sealing the goodness that occurred. I looked over the books that I read so it would sink deeper into my heart and have more of an impression on my memory. I read some of the poems I wrote, some of the prayers I journaled, and some of the Bible passages that were especially important to me. I compiled a list of a few things that God gave me while on sabbatical that I will share with you.

Many of them that I share with you are very, very simple. But without them ministry is miserable.

The Simple Things I Learned

1.   I am thankful for my husband's teaching and leading of our church. In attending other churches, my awareness of his skill and heart was awakened.

2.   Our worship team is amazing. I really missed my church's worship while I was gone.

3.   I missed the people of my church. We have wonderful people.

4.   I don't want to be imprisoned by false beliefs that held so strong before my sabbatical. There is freedom in Christ.

5.   Taking the time for deep friendships is time well spent.

6.   Being brave and asking for what I needed honored God and began a healing in me.

7.   Obedience to Christ is not bound to affirmation or criticism.

8.   God loves me regardless of how people react to my obedience.

9.   There is so much freedom in loving God.

10. God didn't design me by mistake. By living out my life from who I truly am I am honoring him with my life.

11. By not completely being healed of some wounds, I kept repeating some patterns that were sabotaging my calling. I don't want to continue those patterns for another day.

12. Honoring how God has wired me will be good for me, my marriage, my family, and ultimately for Pathways.

13. I can trust my discernment and listening ear to God. And they are closely linked to my deepest longings and desires.

I wanted to share my story because I knew that I couldn't be the only one feeling this way. The exhaustion and stress do not need to be suffered through year after year. Maybe this book will help you see that you do not need to do ministry to the point of burnout. And perhaps it will help you to see signs of exhaustion in your ministry team.

There can be many sustaining benefits to a sabbatical. Perspective, physical wellness, attention to neglected areas of your life, refreshed spiritual maturity and growth, and reduced anxiety and depression are just a few possibilities.

If nothing else, I hope that this book gives you greater empathy and grace for yourself and pastors' families around you.

Isaiah 32:17-18

Doing what is right will bring peace and rest.
When my people do that, they will stay calm
and trust in the Lord forever.
They will live in a peaceful land. Their homes will be secure.
They will enjoy peace and quiet.

Where will God lead you? What will you discover? I would love to hear. You can view free resources, spiritual direction programs, and sabbatical support Tree by Water is offering at *www.treebywater.org,* on Facebook at "Tree by Water," on Twitter at @_treebywater_, or on Instagram at "_treebywater_."

Notes

The Holy Bible, New International Version. (Grand Rapids: Zondervan House, 1984).

Chapter 1

Mark Buchanan, *The Rest of God: Restoring Your Soul by Restoring Sabbath* (Nashville, Tennessee: Thomas Nelson, 2007).

Chapter 2

Shauna Niequist, Bryan Torwalt, and Katie Torwalt. *"Choosing Peace over Perfectionism"* Audio blog post. Catalyst Leadership Podcast. 4 Aug. 2016. Web.

Chapter 3

Alicia Britt Chole, *"Ready, Set, Rest."* (Onewholeworld, Inc., 2014).

Chapter 4

Henry Cloud and John Townsend, *"Boundaries: When to Say Yes, How to Say No."* (Grand Rapids, Michigan: Zondervan, 2021).

Acknowledgements

I wrote this book with the thought that I was going to push past the fear of putting a horrible or simply mediocre book out in the world. There were several people who gave me input that pushed my work further away from horrible. Thank you for your love and affirmation along the way.

Lynda Savage, we sat in your living room and read it out loud over a few mornings. I am positive that the best lines in this book came from the ideas you gave me. You are a brilliant woman, and I thank you for all of the words you have shared with me... the ones that pierced my heart, and the ones that mended it back together.

Teresa Kliner and Alli Godwin, your edits, ideas, and encouragement to keep going were what I needed several days along the way. Thank you!

Adam, thank you for standing up to announce my sabbatical despite your anxiety and fear. From my view, it was one of the finest days in our marriage. I felt protected, valued, and cared for. I love you.

And to my girls, Grace and Ella. You gave me space to read and pray and retreat during my sabbatical, and when I started working on Tree by Water, you cheered me on. I want to live as an example of courage and conviction. In doing so I hope that one outcome is that you feel the confidence to walk the journey you are destined for. Grace, when someone asked you recently to describe your family, the first thing you said was, "My mom is writing a book." You have no idea how much that meant to me.

About Tree by Water

Do you need someone to walk with you in your spiritual journey? Tree by Water is a ministry to create space for growth and healing. Through online spiritual direction, virtual sabbatical support programs, retreats, writing, and prayer, Tree by Water helps people be Rooted In God and True to Themselves. You can connect to Laura and Tree by Water at www.treebywater.org.

About Laura Demetrician

Laura is the Director at Tree by Water, an organization that helps people be "Rooted in God and True to Themselves" through spiritual direction, retreats, and writing. She is a Licensed Marriage and Family Therapist and Certified Spiritual Director. She attended Fuller Theological Seminary and Southeastern University in Lakeland, Florida.

Laura is married to Adam, the Lead Pastor at Pathways Church in Appleton, Wisconsin. They have two daughters, Grace and Ella.

Laura loves hiking, wearing tennis shoes 99% of the time, and enjoying simple beauty in life.